Loretta's Journey Continues

Loretta Knapp

Order this book online at www.trafford.com
or email orders@trafford.com

Most Trafford titles are also available at major online book retailers.

Print information available on the last page.

ISBN: 978-1-4907-6713-0 (sc)
ISBN: 978-1-4907-6712-3 (e)

Trafford rev. 02/09/2016

www.trafford.com
North America & international
toll-free: 1 888 232 4444 (USA & Canada)
fax: 812 355 4082

Contents

I've come a long Way

I'm 54 and I think I've come a long way. You may not see it but I have and I think Pat my therapist would agree with me. I've managed to keep my new apartment for 3 years, I see Pat every 2wks instead of once a week I still sign a no harm contract with her but that's so I don't harm myself in any way like suicide.

Since my mom has been in a nursing home I'm accepting it better and learning to adjust to her illness as well.

A while back my one case worker put me on a budget since then I've been able to save money, before I was living from pay check and till the end of the month I only had a few dollars in my savings account, now its built up.

Another thing I'm doing is volunteering at my church Saint John Gualbert. I enjoy doing it very much it makes me feel good. As I said in my first book I get a chance to talk to Irene and Dorothy two very nice people.

I have a peer specialist and a blended case manager come to my apartment to help me with different things. Pat and my blended case manager say I could become a peer specialist, I say no I still have a hard time handling my problems.

As for my friends I try to keep in touch with them as much as possible, without my friends who know where I'd be.

And then there's my family but I'm always calling them, like the saying goes you can pick your friends, don't get me wrong I like my family but there different.

Taking Medication Has Its Good And Bad Things About It.

For me its helps me cope with my depression, and mood swings, and anxiety. I know I'll be on medication the rest of my life, but that's okay as long as long as it keeps me alive. One thing I don't like about the medicine is the side effects some are weight gain, nausea, loss of appetite, crying hallulation, muscles stiffness, dry mouth and many more, I've had some of these and there not fun. Medication can help you too lead a so called normal life.

For me it consist of getting up in the morning, taking a shower, eating breakfast, wait for my peer specialist Helen to come to do some work, when she leaves I have lunch, go for a walk on a nice day, come home talk to Gale my friend and then my other friend Martha comes up and we talk after she leaves, I usually have supper, and sometimes I walk down to the store for groceries, come home put them away, and watch TV. On Wednesday my blended case manager Lisa, comes to check my medication. On Friday I'm busy in the morning volunteering at my church I get to talk to Dorothy, and Irene. I walk to the Lee Shop for lunch and then come home. Saturday usually wash cloths and clean that day. Sundays I visit my mom at the nursing home.

So you see I am functioning well as long as I stay on my medication. Don't get me wrong I do slip now and then from time to time.

Living With Depression
4-26-12

Living with depression for me has been a rocky road. It can lead to suicide. I've been dealing with it for several years with trying different doctors, therapists, and medication. It takes a lot of work. First I had to be willing to take the medications and deal with the side effects unless they were bad ones like hallucinations and work with them. I also needed to find the right therapist, one who was willing to listen to what I was saying and not just throw me in the hospital for this or that.

In my first book I wrote about my therapist, Pat Hydock, she helps me a lot. She's managed to keep me out of the hospital for several years now, but I sign a no harm contract with her each visit. I'm not allowed to have matches, because when under stress I hear voices to burn myself. I've already took a lighter to my stomach. I still have the scar.

Ways I cope with my depression are to seek out for my support team, keep myself busy, work on my cross-stitch, clean my apartment, go for a walk, treat myself to a new CD, or lunch, call Gale and do something fun. There are days I still get depressed and don't want to get out of bed, but I force myself.

Right now I have a reason. Helen my Peer Star is coming and helping me organizing my apartment and she makes me happy. She's supportive.

My blended case manager comes one day. Lisa checks things I don't understand, my medication refills, takes me to my doctor appointments.

My depression comes and goes for instance holiday's anniversaries, and birthdays of the death of my dad and grandmother. The winter season I guess my point to this story is there is hope I'm here to prove it. Depression is treatable.

When People Ask Me How Am I?
10-2-12

My most and usually response is I'm hanging in there, you can take it two ways. Such as I'm okay, I'm living. Never I'm good, or I'm fine, also, I'm taking it easy. But I always ask how they are doing.

People don't want to hear your problems I try to be opened minded for suggestions, and I find myself listening to other people's problems. It's my nature to help and care for friends, that's just my personality. I like sharing my crafts with people who have feelings and care about me that's my way of saying thank you.

Some days I'd like to crawl in a corner or not even get out of bed it's like pulling teeth, to function from day to day. I put myself down and get into a depression.

My support team really comes through and pulls me out and gets me functioning again, they give me courage and strength to move on.

When I think about it I'm an okay person. I'm fighting a mental illness problem and battling a weight problem

Life
11-26-12

For me every day is a different experience, example. When I wake up in the morning I take a shower, and it depends on the weather and mood if I decide to take a walk to the Lee Shop and have breakfast and talk to the women at the shop. I consider them my friends and part of my support team.

While I'm over there I'll stop at the credit union to get money out, I have friends there Marybeth, Connie, Sharon, Ruth, they also I consider a part of my support team.

On another nice day I'll take a walk to the grocery store. Looking at me can you tell I need to eat, ha' ha'.

I have other days that are planed out for me like my Peer Star Helen comes in the morning from 9 till 1, it's an experience having her help me so much, like organizing my apartment, going for walks, going shopping, socializing, and problem solving, that's only part of it.

Then I have a blended case manager that comes once a week, she takes me to my doctor appointments, helps me when my medication needs to be filled, and papers I don't understand

And then I do have a day set aside when I do laundry, and clean the apartment, I do have plenty of experience in that department. I almost forgot my volunteering job at Saint Johns Church, I love my job and the people there, like Irene and Dorothy, they help me out, there friendly they give me water and candy, and they talk to me, they too I consider my support team.

On Sundays I visit my mom in the nursing home with my best friend Gale. When we leave my mom we go to McDonalds.

My nice and pleasant experience is when I go to the North Fork Dam, I said it in my first book and I'll say it in my 2nd book.

Another example is the seasons, let's start first with fall. I enjoy watching the leaves change their colors at this time I like going out to the North Fork Dam it's relaxing, and it's my special place.

Thanksgiving is in the fall and my friend Gale and I spend that day together, we have turkey and all the trimmings.

Winter isn't a good time for me it's usually dark when you get up and the same way when you go to bed. I usually isolate myself, I'm depressed. This is the time I depend on Pat Hydock, and my support team.

Christmas is nice, Gale and I spend that holiday together, we have ham and all the trimmings, and we have a good time.

New Year's Gale comes to my place and we celebrate that night together we have fun, we have kolbossie, sauerkraut, crackers and cheese it's nice. We watch the fireworks and then go to bed.

Spring is nice all the flowers start to bloom, the air smells fresh, birds are singing. And the only fault there is allergy season.

Then comes summer time it's a time for planting flowers, and vegetables, and cutting grass. It's bad for me with my allergies.

No matter what happens to me I know I have a support team.

What Does Watching and
Playing a Sport Mean TO Me
3-12-2013

For me it's a challenge. You play as a team and it's a team effort, I was always out for the fun of the game, not out for blood, sure I wanted to win the game, if our team won the game I was happy and so were my team mates and the coach, if we lost the game we were sad and mad and that meant practice harder.

I enjoyed sports in grade school I played basketball and soccer. After I graduated I joined a women's volleyball league I really enjoyed that even though we didn't win any games I had fun doing it, and it got me and my sister out for fun in the evening.

I also enjoy watching sports on TV, like women's and men's soccer, and volleyball, beach volleyball is fun but I don't like how they sweat and the sand sticks to their body. Golf I like a little bit, it's about competition always trying to do better than the other team but at the end may the best team win

Signing off ESPN

D0 I Like This Person Who She Really Is
5-8-13

It all depends on how you look at me; you can see me two ways negative, and positive. Some people see me as a mental or sick person. While others look at me as a normal person.

What matters is how I do really like me for who I am? The answer to that is sometimes yes and sometimes no.

I see me as a 54 yr. old woman soon to turn 55 and scared. I'm a person with a mental illness which stops me from growing. I reach out for help my problems and now I have a good support team that help me my tough times, I need now mention their names because there throughout my book.

I've come a long way I'm still living on my own, in my apt, I keep up with my hygiene, I have a car I pay my own bills I have a volunteer job once a week I take my medication the way I'm supposed to, I'm friendly and sometimes I get shy and backwards.

The negative things about me is I worry a lot, I'm over weight, which is a constant battle, I'm suicidal, that's not too bad, just those few things.

While I was 54 I managed publish a book, hopefully when I'm 55, I'll publish another book

Part of me likes who I really see the other part has and still needs work on. There's is still hope for improvement all the time, just look around and see.

Mental illness

Mental illness is something that's not talked about much. For me my mental illness started at an early age. It's something you don't treat lightly like a cut you put a band aide on it and it will go away. It doesn't work that way. You need help.

I see how people look at me some of them see me as a normal person, but they don't know what's going on inside my head, like my mind just keeps racing when I'm under stress, and that I do have problems. And there are others who see me as a crazy person and are afraid to talk to me.

But I can show those people with the help of a doctor to give me medication and Pat Hydock my therapist they can keep me on track, don't get me wrong I have mood swings and anxiety at times. I can lead a somewhat normal life and I have a support team I can reach out to.

I'm able to maintain my apartment, keep up with my hygiene, care for other people, do my crafts, drive my car, volunteer, pay my own bills, and manage my own money.

Christmas 2012

Let's see for me it started in the month of Nov, buying gifts, and getting money together that I saved to give my nieces and nephews for Christmas as there gift from me.

The month of December I wrote out my Christmas cards out in the beginning of the month and sent them out with the help of Helen my peerstar.

I was depressed most of the month of December due to my mental illness. I was hearing voices and seeing things, and crying a lot. I probably drove my brother Ken and my friends Debbie and Gail crazy calling them a lot I was even talking to Pat. But I was reaching out to my support team. Pat says it's the holidays that put stress on me, and it's the season. The other thing that has me down is I'm never ready for Christmas, and this year I was ready the first week in December and that's not me.

I did see the doctor on the 20th she just increase my one pill for anxiety just until the holidays are over. I went to my volunteer job on Friday Irene and Dorothy gave me a big basket with gifts and I gave them theirs they cheered me up.

Christmas Eve Helen and I went to McDonalds and then came back to my apartment and talk. I cried a little but they were happy and sad tears.

Later in the day Megan came and I cried some more I signed a no harm contract she gave me a nice Christmas card. I keep telling myself I'll be okay. I did wash a load of cloths.

Martha my friend came up and I ordered a small pizza for us. I gave her a Christmas card with a gift in it. She was a little happy. She stayed till 7:30.

Then I open two of my gifts and started to cry so I stopped. I figured out I should wait till my friend Gale comes tomorrow.

Christmas time should be a happy time Jesus was born, the wise men brought gifts. Families get together give presents to one another, and eat a lot of food.

But for me it's a little different my sister invites me to her house for Christmas, she don't understand as long as my mom is living in the nursing home I'm going to spend time with her. And then I have my friend Gale we've been spending the holidays together for a couple years now and we have a good time.

This year one thing changed Gale and I weren't able to visit my mom at the nursing home there was outbreak of a virus so we couldn't take a chance of getting it. But I still picked up Gale and we did our thing. Put the ham loaf in the oven, while that was baking Gale and I opened our gifts, we were happy with them.

We watch some TV, and then it was time to finish off the dinner, like the stuffing, and sweet potatoes. We did pretty well, food was good, we saved the best for last Christmas cookies that Janice Forry and Gale made that tasted great. I did up the dishes and Gale watched TV.

Later that evening Gale and I went down to Martha's to ask her to come up and she came up later. We had fun listening to her stories. When Martha went home at 8:00 Gale went to bed and I watched TV and fell asleep. One thing I did forget to mention is most of my brothers and sisters called to wish me a merry Christmas except for my brother Paul and sister Tammy.

All in all I did have a merry Christmas for the year 2012. I may have shed some tears but they were both happy and sad tears. MERRY CHRISTMAS

New Year 2013

New Year's 2013 came upon me very quickly. How did I spend the last day of 2012 I woke up and called the dentist and told Shryle about my tooth and started to cry, she told me not to worry and call back if I needed to talk.

Next thing to happen was for Helen my peerstar person to show up at 11:15 we made arrangements to go for some groceries, she took me in her car, good thing it was freezing out there we would have frozen our butts off carrying them home. When we came home we talk and then we took my tree down and my nativity set down and packed it away. By then it was time for Helen to leave we accomplished a lot.

Megan my blended case manager called earlier and said she wouldn't be able to come but she could come Wednesday.

Soon the fun was going to begin I was going to pick Gale my friend up so we could start to party. But first I had to pick up two double cheeseburgers for my friend Martha. We came home and I dropped off the cheeseburgers at Martha's and then the fun began. We were watching TV and the phone rang it was my niece Julie she asked if she could stop by, I said sure. So then I cut up cheese and meat and put out some crackers and a tray of cookies. When Julie came she gave me a bouquet of flowers there really nice. She talked and we laughed and we ate, we had a good time. When Julie left I put the kolbossie and sourkaurt on. Gale and I made a sandwich and when we were done I did up the dishes.

All we had to do is wait for the ball to drop it seemed like a long time only two hours. While we were waiting we saw some fireworks outside my living room window Gale was really amazed. When they were over it was back to the TV Gale kept dozing off but the two of us did see the ball drop and we blew our horns. So we did manage to ring in the year 2013.

We went to bed, I got up at 7:20am to put the pork and sourkaurt in the oven made coffee and then went back to bed. Gale and I woke up around 9:00 had breakfast. It was like pulling teeth to get Gale to take a shower, but she did. After she took hers I took mine.

Mrs. Forry called and told us about the parade on TV so were watching that. We had dinner at noon and did up the dishes again.

When the parade was over I took Gale home I swear when she comes to sleep over my place I should get a U-Haul. We had a good time.

When I came home I just relaxed and later went down to Martha's she was cleaning so I didn't stay long. Later Martha came up and talked same old stuff I just let her talk. After she left I had a little supper.

Oh I almost forgot my brother John called me yesterday to tell me Happy New Year, and today my brother Ken called and wished me Happy New Year.

My New Year's resolution is giving up sugar I know I can do it. I have faith and I did it before. I hope I have happy New Year and all those around me.

Pastor Forry and Janice Forry
1-4-13

They're the most nicest and pleasant people I've come to know. I met them through my good friend Gale. They opened their house up to me one weekend to spend it with Gale to.

Pastor Forry is a funny man and a respectful man he tells me to call him Roger but I have a hard time doing that, sometimes I'll call him Roger without thinking and other times I'll call him Pastor Forry out of respect. Now for some reason I don't have hard time calling Janice Forry-Janice.

When Gale and I have spent a weekend up at the Forrys I've really had a nice time. Janice keeps us moving. We do meals on wheels, Gale got a haircut. Or one day Gale and I walk down to the Christian book store Gale could spend all day at the store. We eat meals there and do dishes all that sort of stuff but its fun.

At meal time Roger is always telling us stories which are nice to hear sometimes there religious and sometimes it's about him growing up. After that we watch TV or sit on the porch and watch chipmunks run around and the kids play.

Just this past year Roger and Janice have been blessed with two granddaughters named Allison and Sara.

When 9 o'clock or 9:30 comes around I'm ready for bed. Lately that's been a problem Gale saws wood all night if you don't know what that means she snores.

When Sunday morning comes around Gale takes a shower and then I get one. After that we pack our bags and then have breakfast, sometimes Pastor Forry is there and sometimes not he sometimes has to preach at a different church. So that leaves Janice Forry and Gale and I to go to

Christopher their son's church that's okay I like it. It's different from my church but I understand it they sing Janice can sing

I hate to burst your bubble Gale you need a little more practice. After church Janice takes us out to eat and we meet Roger we have a good time. We come home to rest awhile and then Janice brings us back home. I really have a good time with Roger and Janice Forry they have become my friends.

Addictions
1-21-2013

There are a number of kinds of addiction. I know I'm speaking from experience I have 5, sugar, weight pills, burning and cutting. My biggest battle with sugar was m&ms I could eat them by the pound plain and peanut. I haven't had an m&m for at least 15 yrs. or longer. I can't say I miss them but I lost weight when I quit eating them I know just one m&m would take me off track. I'm proud of myself for doing this.

Also on January 1, 2013 I cut out sugar I'm trying to kill two birds with one stone; I'm hoping to lose weight at the same time. So far it's the 21st and I haven't had any sugar. It takes a lot of willpower and praying to God. You also have to watch what you eat. I have a confession to make something I'm not proud of it but when I was still living at home and trying to lose weight I was stealing my grandmothers Lasix she was prescribed 20mg a day and sometimes she would skip a day or two so I would take 40mg I sure went to the bathroom a lot I did that for a short period of time because I started to feel funny but I did lose the weight.

Next I turned to laxatives there again I went to the bathroom a lot, but that didn't matter I was losing weight.

Even after that I still wasn't happy I bought a bottle of epiaket syrup that stuff was nasty I don't even want to tell you what that made me do but I'm sure you can figure that one out for yourself. So I apologized for taking grandmas pills.

Now 2013 I'm on the right track for my sugar free diet and its working nobody's going stop me.

Let's move on before I went for treatment I had an addiction of burning and cutting myself. Every time I got mad I'd either take a knife and cut my arm or a lighter and burn my arm. If someone hurt my feelings or laughed at me I'd do one or the other.

Now I have voices telling me to cut myself or burn myself.

So you see I'm working hard on my recovery from my addiction there are other addictions worse than mine but I can only control myself.

Dad
2-3-2013

Well dad today is your 18th anniversary since you pasted away. I miss you as though it was today. I still see you walking in the bank and I'm telling myself I'll pick you up on my way home from groceries shopping but it took me longer than I thought so I figured you would be home. But when I got home I got a call from John to come up to the house. So when I went up to the house they told me you pasted away I cried I tried to be strong but I couldn't.

My therapist told me it would have been bad if I would have been in the bank that day.

But dad you were laid out nice and looked good. The day of your funeral the weather was bad we had a bad sleet and snow storm.

I still miss you very much, I hope you're looking down at me and seeing how much I've achieved in life, since you left me.

Your loving daughter
Loretta

My Fantasy of What Heaven Would Look Like If I Make It There
2-13-2013

First I would have to die and get buried. Then I think I was a good Christian as best to my knowledge.

But I see myself rising up into the beautiful sky with some angles with their wings and holding out there hands guiding up into the gates of heaven, where God will be waiting there with his hands open wide saying come to me.

I'll be so happy because I'll be with my grandma my dad, some of my other relatives, and some of my friends that have passed away. I'll be with tiger my cat and all the other pets I've had growing up as a child and as an adult.

I picture it with a beautiful sky always sunshine, and everyone getting along. I don't know about you but I think that I would like it in heaven it would also be a resting place, and a peaceful place that will be my next home.

Hearing Voices
3-21-2013

As you may recall in my first book I wrote there was a story on hearing voices. Well at this time I'm experiencing voices and they're very strong telling me time is running out. For me it means my life is coming to an end. I'm fighting it the best way I can I've called my friends, I've reached out to my support team, I've even tried calling my doctor to get an increase in my medicine, but they told me the doctor is away for a couple of weeks, and if they increased the trilafon I might have a bad side effect so they don't want to do that.

So I'm trying to use some coping skills like keeping busy, watching TV, going for walks to the Lee Shop and spending time with the ladies there, and like I said earlier reaching out to my friends and my support team.

All that's going through my mind is I don't have my book finished and I don't have my plot paid for or my stone bought.

Right now I feel like leaving a suicide note, part of me knows it's not the answer but I don't know what else to do.

I'm Sorry

I want to thank Pat Hydock for all the time you spent with me. You help me out a lot in many ways so don't blame yourself for my death, God wouldn't want you to do that and I wouldn't want that either.

As for my family sigh in relief you don't have to worry about me any more I won't be a problem anymore. I'm one less thing you have to worry about. Please make sure all the nieces and nephews get a panda bear. I apologize that left you to pay for the rest of my plot and stone. I hope to have all my other bills paid off.

Now to my friends and my support team I treasured every moment we spent together we shared a lot of good times. I'll never forget you. Just keep in your mind I'm at peace now and no more fighting.

Having a Support Team
4-5-13

Having a support team is important to me. It's someone I can reach out for help when I'm feeling down and need to talk to.

It doesn't always mean you can only talk to them when feeling down you can also talk to them when you're feeling good.

I have a good and well balanced support team it consist of Pat Hydock my therapist, my peer star Helen, my blended case manager Meagan, my friend Gale, Debbie, Connie Marybeth Sharon Ruth. The ladies at the credit union, the ladies at the lee shop and of course Pastor Forry and Janice, they are always so nice to me. Sheryl from Dr. Bach's, Irene, Dorothy from church where I volunteer their always nice and friendly to me on Fridays. Annamary, my brother Ken my niece Julie, I can always call them to talk to.

These supporters are all good to me and I'm there for them. Without them I wouldn't be where I'm at today. So thank you all from the bottom of my heart and God Bless.

Some Things I Have To Learn To Live With
4-14-2013

One major thing is my mental illness I have to deal with it the rest of my life. Believe me it's not easy. And especially if you are diagnosed with schizoaffective disorder. I mentioned it once before what it is but I'll tell you again, it's when you have mood swings highs and lows once in a while I'm on an even keel, I constantly fight with voices every day, when I'm under stress there louder and other days there not so bad but still there.

I'm on medication for them; part of my mental illness is depression and anxiety I'm also on medication for that to. But I can't depend on the medication to do all the work. I have to learn to live with it and cope with it. By that I mean use some relaxation technique keep myself busy, go for walks, talk to my support team, pray, and take the medication as prescribed.

I sometimes think it's my mental illness is what I'm going to die from. And yet on the other hand I feel it's going to be my physical illness. I have arthritis in my hands and knees and I try not to let it get me down. I take medication and continue to walk even though its hurts I keep going. And I have other physical problems I don't feel comfortable talking about it. I think that's what is going to take me.

I don't know which is harder to deal with mental illness
or physical pain maybe it amounts equal.

Finding Yourself
04-17-2013

How to go about finding yourself First of all I think you have to start off by looking deep within yourself and check things out. It's not going to be easy but you have to take that chance. The outcome might not be as bad as you thought it would be.

So let's start with me, I look in the mirror for a few minutes and I find myself as an individual with a mental illness and have problems in her life. I also see that part of me is a survivor.

I also see me living independently for several years now I've had help along the way and I'm not embarrassed to admit it.

I take care of my hygiene, cleaning, cooking, paying bills on time, my health, friendly, I volunteer one day a week at my church.

I like to watch TV, I'm a loner. I don't handle pressure very well. I'm a person with feelings that sometimes get hurt. I'm a happy person.

I constantly am worrying about my weight. I pray a lot.

Trying to write this one story was more like a chore but the outcome isn't bad because I have people around me who care. Finding myself made me think a lot.

The outcome is I'm 54 yrs. old and I'm not a bad person, and I can keep on searching.

Functioning With Mental Illness
4-23-13

For me it's been a long and narrow path in my life. I function with a mental illness for a period of time I've grown from it. By that I mean.

I've learn to accept it as part of my life. I'm independent and living on my own I have an apartment, I take care of my hygiene, I clean my apartment, I cook I've learned to budget my money, *I'm* friendly, I keep myself busy when I'm depressed I go for walks, I visit my mom in the nursing home, I volunteer at the church once a week, I go to the Lee shop, I go to the credit union, I see Pat Hydock every other week.

And I see my Peer Star Helen and a Blended Case Manager Megan, and I keep my doctor's appointments they keep me functioning, I pray a lot.

I find myself wakening up in the morning and saying oh shit another day and other day's I wake up and say Thank You God and go about my business.

It took me a long time to get where I'm at today. I still could be functioning a little better but with some support I'll get there. There's hope for me and I know there's hope for my other friends.

DO I like this person for who she really is?
05-08-2013

It all depends on how you look at me; you can see me two ways negative and positive. Some people see me as a mentally sick person. While others look at me as a normal person.

What matters is how I really like me for who I am? The answer to that is sometimes yes and sometimes no.

I see me as a 54 yr. old woman soon to turn 55 and scared. I am a person with a mental illness which stops me from growing. I reach out for help for my problems and now I have a good support team that help me through the tough times, I do not need to mention their names because throughout my book.

I've come a long way I'm still living on my own in my apt#. I keep up with my hygiene, I have my own car, I pay my own bills, have a volunteer job once a week, I take my medication the way I'm supposed to, I'm friendly and sometimes I get shy and backward.

The negative things about me are I worry a lot, I'm over weight which is a constant battle and I'm suicidal, that's not too bad, just those few things. While I was 54 I manage to publish a book when I'm 55 I hope to publish another one.

Part of me likes who I really see; the other part has or still needs work on. There's still hope for improvement all the time, just look around and see.

How Gale and I Became Friends
5-9-13

Well it was in the year 2003. I was taking a Peer to Peer class, it was held down at the Drop in Center. I was nervous my first day and on top of that I was a half hour early and didn't know what to expect. So I sat on a chair and waited.

Then comes in this woman with a bear and a lunch box and sat down beside me. I thought to myself what did I get myself into now.

The group started with an introduction of names when it came to this lady she introduce herself as Gale and then she also introduce her bears name Max. There was at least ten other people in the group, but out of all of them Gale and Max and I connected the whole time.

For lunch I packed crackers and a soda Gale had a sandwich, fruit, and milk, I shared my crackers with her.

Then Gale asks me if I'd walk her up to the MH-MR building she didn't know how to get there so I said sure. I was going that way anyhow, so we walk and talk together and got to know each other.

When the next week came Gale brought me a sandwich and I gave her a gob and some crackers. We shared lunches. We walked to the building together again. The Classes lasted for ten weeks.

I had some groups I was attending so after my group I'd wait for Gale and we would have lunch. When my groups ended we exchanged phone numbers and addresses I went to her apartment and she came to mine. We have a good friendship she helped me when I had back surgery, my hysterectomy. When it was time for me to move to my new apartment Gale help me out a lot so did my family moving day. Gale recently sent me a note card in it said I can learn a lot from you like common sense, and self-control but Gale helps me in other ways.

What can I say Gales a Good friend and my Best friend.

When Gale moved to Loughner Plaza we became closer I'd invite her to family picnics, parties and she'd invite me to actives at her apartment.

When I could really trust Gale I took her to my special place. It got to where now we spend holidays together.

Recovery
6-1-13

Recovery is something I'm always striving for. But it seem from time to time I find myself relapse.

Right now I'm dealing with a lot of anxiety in my life and how am I being treated for it an increase with one more medication. Am I happy with it no, but it's for the best, to keep me out of the hospital. I know it's not a permanent fix and when my anxiety level goes down they will decrease it, when that will be I don't know.

The cards are laid on table as one would say it's more or less up to me and my doctor.

I'm surrounded by people who are willing to help me with what's causing my anxiety but it's going to take time and patience.

I won't be in recovery for a couple of months. I just have to accept it and hope for the best outcome my medication will be back to normal and I'll be more myself.

Hope
6-4-13

Having hope is something I cling or hang onto. Without having hope and a support team I wouldn't be here. I have hope that someday they will find a cure for mental illness, and that one day voices in my head would go away.

My support team sees me as a strong person, but there wrong, again without their help I would not survive. As of today June 4, 2013 I have little hope I'm not so sure I can bounce back to the happy Loretta, always caring, and looking out for the other person, that's just not me. My hope is hanging on a thin thread.

No I'm not being selfish. I know there are other people besides me that have hope, for example people with cancer are always hoping they find a cure so they may live, and yet every day you see in the newspaper so and so passed away from cancer, and donate to the hospice foundation.

IN this case hope is a strong word use it wisely when you say it, and when you think it.

When Debbie and I Became Friends, 6-13-13

We first met in the year 1974 at Greater Johnstown Vo- Tech We were in the same home room and our lockers were close together,

We gradually started to talk to one another and exchanged phone numbers,

Debbie was studying to be a health nurse health related technology she was very smart, one thing about Debbie is if she wanted something bad enough she'd get it one way or another. She's a strong willed person, I was more laid back.

Debbie and I would go for walks and we would talk about our problems and school. I would meet her part way and we would stop at Sheetz for a drink and then we talk some more, then it would be time for us to go our separate ways for the night. I remember after Debbie graduated x-ray technician and she got a car and named it Ginger.

And one Saturday Debbie took her sister Susan and I horseback riding that was fun.

But before I forget there was a boy Mark in high school that liked Debbie. I worked hard to get them together. They had their rocky roads splitting up not talking and then back together. After a couple of years they did get married, they had two boys that are grown up and doing well.

And Debbie and I have been able to keep in touch with each other over the years and still remain best friends and hope it continues on for many more.

How My Mom Would Want Us To Remember Her By

To start off she would like to remember the time she put seven kids first, before herself. And how many times she did without.

She always made sure we had clean cloths. And as we grew up in school she tried to show up for our sports games, it wasn't easy.

My mom made also made sure we were well fed with the help of my father.

My mom was also famous for her potato salad when it came to holidays and picnics she always made potato salad.

Then came a time when she took care of her mother, she deserves a medal for that. Her mother lived to be 95 years old.

She worked for a period of time until she got dementia.

Let me take a couple steps back my mom belonged to St Columbus Ladies Guild for several years that was something she enjoyed and got her out of the house. She cooked for the church dinners.

She took some trips to Virginia Beach to see her son and family and to Falls Church Virginia to visit her daughter and family, and then she went to Camp Hill to visit her daughter and family. She took bus trips while she could until dementia set in.

My sister Barb and her husband took her in and gave her proper care that she needed until she got too bad.

She lived in the Presbyterian Home where she was getting more care that we couldn't give her. My mom was a happy and talkative person, and now she can't do that, she has a feeding tube in her. I know she's not a happy camper in the place but we had no choice.

Now she's in a resting place and not suffering no more. MAY YOU REST IN PEACE AND BE HAPPY. WE LOVE YOU.

A Cry for Help
7-5-13

Sometimes I need help at night when I'm having a crisis and feel the need to talk to my support team before I think of harming myself.

I call Pat Hydock my therapists after working hours with her she has a way of calming me down.

I call my friend Gale and we talk for maybe an hour or more and she says a prayer for me, she may not know what to say but she just listens. I'll call her two o clock in the morning to read a story I just wrote and she gets excited, and tell me if she likes it. I can always count on Gale, she's my best friend.

I can count on calling my friend Debbie I usually call her through the day, but lately it's been at night, like she says to me she may not know what to say, but she's there for me to listen to. The door swings both ways when she calls me with problems I just listen to that what friends are for. She also is my best friend.

I also have permission to call my Peer Star Helen when I need to we check in with each other about every night, even though she seen me that day we check in its helpful for me. She's pulled me out of some crisis situations. She's been one of the best Peer Star specialist that I've had.

What puts me in a crisis that I need a support team, things my family do, just everyday living, physical and emotion problem, voices. I need those people I mention above to pull me through this crisis without them I wouldn't be here today so thanks to all of you.

I also want to mention my brother Ken I sometimes call him and he just listens and says he wishes there was something he could do. I mainly call him when the voices are bad and I'm ready to give in. He's there for me and we keep in touch. So thanks again for all your support.

Loretta's Not A Little Girl Any More
7-10-13

Yes that's what I said I'm not a little girl anymore. I'm soon to be 55 yrs. old. Why do people or family members put this shield up and keep things from me. Are they afraid they're going to hurt me well it hurts me more when they keep things from me.

I don't need protected anymore sure I still have mental illness but don't let that stop you. I'm fighting with it every day but I have a support team and I use coping skills.

If I was a little girl I wouldn't be out on my own, I wouldn't pay my bill, clean my apartment, keep up with my hygiene, keep up with my doctors' appointments, drive car, have friends.

I'm Loretta who has feelings and gets hurt, but I'm asking for a chance for everyone to share things with me good or bad, and stop being so over protective. I may fall or crash but with a support system and coping skills I just might bounce right up. We will never know unless you try. Remember I'm not that little girl anymore. I'm Loretta.

Life Has ITS Moments
8-4-13

Just what do I mean by that? Well we have our good days and our bad days. Happy moments and not so happy moments. There are people out there that take life for granted.

Now for me I'm one of these people who have to take one day at a time and live minute to minute. Due to my illness being schizoaffective I'm like a roller coaster going up and down, hardly ever on an even keel. I think of suicide from time to time when things are getting out of control. Then that's when my support team comes in I don't have to name them because I have them written throughout my book.

I'm one I don't like to take risk, or try new things. I don't like crowds. I like to make people happy example when I walk into the credit union Connie, Marybeth, Sharon, Ruth always have a smile on their face and make me laugh, but we have our own little secret between us, it makes laugh for a few minutes while I'm there.

My friend Gale has me laugh for a moment when she calls me a silver foxete#1. The ladies at the Lee Shoppe come up with some funny stuff to when I'm there. Pat Haydock makes me laugh every time I think of her green poke a dot nightgown just those few moments of happiness make me feel good and it should make you feel good too. Remember just because I can't take things for granted don't mean you should stop.

Soon to be 55
8-21-2013

Two more days and I'll turn 55 yrs. old. I'm a little hesitated on it; I'm not as sure if I want to see 55. I'm depressed.

I look back at being 54 and what things I might have accomplished. Two good things are I started writing a 2nd book, and I managed to continue my volunteer job at Saint Johns Church, I enjoy it very much I like seeing Irene and Dorothy.

Other things are my dentist made a partial for my bottom teeth it's only a part of one.

I'm still living on my own in my apartment, paying my bills on time, keeping up with my hygiene. Keeping my Dr. Appointment even though I need some assistance. I'm still watching my weight that will be a Constant battle. I still go see my mom at the nursing home which is hard.

I'm sure glad I have a good support system and I see Pat Hydock every other week and Helen sometimes 3 or 4 times a week and Megan 2 times a week. I talk to my best friend Gale a couple times a day and we do things on Sunday. I talk to my other best friend Debbie every other week. Today is the Aug 21st I'm very depressed and having a hard time finding my accomplishments. I have other things working on my mind. Pleased forgive me Every Year I make it, another hurdle I've jumped over.

Eulogy for My Brother John
9-02-2013

What I want to say about my brother John. He was the oldest out of seven of us.

Speaking from my other brothers and sisters we all look up to him. If I had a problem or didn't understand medical papers I always gave them to John to have him read them and explain them to me.

I know Janet would say he was a good husband to her. And Ryan would say he was a good father to him.

Something we all knew John was he like trains, and his nieces and nephews enjoyed coming to the house to see Johns display of trains and watch the train run. We will miss that.

John also enjoyed bowling on a Tuesday night league with his wife. When he had time in the summer he would try and get a game of golf in. He was an active member of the Knight of Columbus for years.

He was employed at Lee Hospital and then Conamaugh Memorial Hospital when they took over.

He served in the United States Army for 4 years.

We will all miss him very much and we are proud that he was our brother, a good husband and father.

Grieving
9-2 13

Grieving everyone handles it differently. Some may grieve the first or 2nd week the person is deceased. And others it may take longer.

For me I cry every day for my brother it's been 3wks. Just when I'm having a good day someone comes up to me and says there sorry about my brother, and it starts everything all over again.

You see I looked up to my brother John for different things, for instance I had his name on my check book, I had him in case of an emergency to contact him, I had him read papers I didn't understand, and most important of all my beneficiary. That all change and people know who know me know I don't accept change very well.

And my grieving process isn't going to mend overnight. It's going to take months maybe a year or longer. First I have to let myself cry, get angry, pray, and continue taking my medication and therapy with Pat Hydock and talk about it. Stick to my support system. And try very hard not to go into depression, and isolate myself. I have to be patient and deal with the grieving process.

Other members of my family seemed to move on with their life. I'm not saying there not grieving but there dealing with it better them me.

Thank God for my friend Gale she slept over night at my apt a week after my brother passes away and now I have her say a prayer every night before I go to bed to keep me safe. I still cry myself to sleep but that's a good thing, that's a part of the grieving process. In time I hope to be back on my feet and back to myself.

Noah Built an Ark
10-6-13

Yes I recall Noah building an ark because God told him to. When he was done with the ark he gathered up animals 2 by 2 of a kind. Then came the flood came the flood, for me I think God had Noah built the ark for me to for the flood but for the flood of tears I shed. By now the ark should be over flowed, for as much as I have cried. I cried for many reasons not only the loss of my brother, but for my grandparents, my father, my aunt, for the loss of the therapist that I had, and for the friends I've lost, I cry for my mother who is at the nursing home I cry for the loss of my cat tiger.

God doesn't want me to cry over sad things so much. I do have happy times far and few in-between. Some of my happy times are when I spend time with Gale, when Helen comes we work on goals and go to McDonalds and the Lee Shoppe When Megan blended case manager comes, when I go to the credit union, and when I see Pat Hydock and we talk about my problems and she gives me guidance. All of the above give me support and help me on the road to recovery. Recovery plays a big part in my life.

So next time you think of Noah's Ark and the flood, take time and stop and think about Loretta's ark, Noah was a good man.

Faith Hope and Love
10-12-13

Where am I going with these three strong words? Well I grew up on them I was raised a catholic and went to a catholic school up to the 10 grade. So you know where I'm going, all I heard pray this have faith and God will help you, have hope and give it some time God will see you through, and then there's love one another and I will love you.

Growing up with faith there were times in my life I lost my faith. Sure I was what you would call a good catholic I was baptized made my first communion, conformation. And after that I'd say when I went downhill for a while.

I lost faith and didn't see any hope and love was a dirty word. You see I had a nervous breakdown and didn't want to do anything, stop going to church for a couple of months, and I closed off to the world. The voices were terrible. I gave up on hope thinking I couldn't be helped. I lost my job things just got worse. My mom kept me up at her house till I got back on my feet, then I went back to my apartment. I applied for social security and was lucky and got back on my medication.

If it wasn't for my dad I'd still be laying on the couch he stopped down at my apartment and said were going for a walk and get a cup of coffee so I did we did it a couple of times.

Then a couple months went by and I decided to give God another chance on faith and went back to church, I went in the back room. I guess there's still hope for me.

Now I volunteer at St Johns church once, but I don't go to church I watch it on TV.

I have love in my heart but when it comes to men I think their dirty one of the men RAPED me. Not too many people know about it only certain people know, I don't like talking about it. I should have reported it, but I was scared. I'm scared for life. I can't love a man any more.

I'm having a hard time getting over my brother death but with Faith, Hope, Love, will get me through.

Having Mental Illness Is
Hard To Live With

I know that from speaking from experience I've been dealing with it for a long time you ask Pat Hydock. It's like you're given a label I have schizoaffective.

Some people look at me as a sick person and afraid to talk to me that includes family, friends, relatives,. But as time has gone and they read my first book and learned about me there making some progress and treat me a little better, they still have some work to do there not out of the woods yet.

Yes I have work on my own to deal with living every day with voices, doing daily things like getting out of bed, taking my medication, keeping up with my hygiene, cleaning, helping and caring for others, going to doctors' appointments, visiting my mom in the nursing home, keep doing my volunteer job at the church, pay my bills on time, stay in touch with my family, friends, and support team and pray. Some people can't do that.

Living with a mental illness is no picnic it's a chore for me some days. I don't deal with change very well, but neither do normal people. It takes me longer to make decisions then other people, I don't understand directions right away, as someone else might, I need them explained to me, but as time goes by with the help of Helen I'm gradually improving.

Living with my mental illness isn't easy but people who are normal it's not so for them either, they have their fault to, they have a way of hiding it. People with mental illness it's hard to hide, I try to hide mine but people see it in my eyes and face, what can I say or do?

Sleep
11-28-13

What's that? I've been asking myself that question for months now. Yah sure I can blame it on my illness, that they diagnosed me as the holidays, racing thoughts missing my brother who passed away on September 3rd 2013, for over a month. I think all that is enough to keep a person awake.

I know I take on a lot of responsibility with my friend Martha, but I'm starting to put my foot down with her.

When I bring it up to my doctor about me not sleeping they say I have too much going on and they don't what to change my medicine, because I'm doing so well on it and if they increase it I'll be a zombie and I won't be able to function. There right and I don't what that. They also told me a person my age only needs 5 hours of sleep; I agree with them there because I'm able to get up in the morning and do things, like take a shower and everyday things. Once in a while I'm dragging and by 2pm I'm ready to sleep for a half hour but that's all.

To some people I guess they need their sleep. But for me I just stay awake and worry, cry, or just watch TV. I'll sign off for now sleep tight and sweet dreams.

Christmas
12-28-13

Christmas of 2013 was different and a difficult for me, I take that back it wasn't just hard for me but for my other brothers, and sisters, but it was harder on me because I'm single and the other members of the family are married. What I'm trying to say it this is the first Christmas without my oldest brother John, who passed away September 3rd 2013. I've been really struggling with that, I've had to depend on my support team and they know who they are.

MY sister Barb and I baked cookies which was good. Christmas eve I cried. But thanks God for Pastor Forry and Janice they came and took Gale and me up to their house in Somerset Christmas day. We spent the day and part of the evening with Janice and Rogers's family which took my mind off my mother and brother for a while. The family treated me very nice and had a gift for me. When we got back home to go to bed it hit me I cried a little bit I just went out and watched some TV with Janice.

Gale and I woke up at 7:30 took a shower had breakfast. We just sat around the table and talked till 12pm. Roger had to get ready for therapy, so Janice took us to Burger King then we dropped Roger off for therapy and took Gale and me to the Christian book store. Gale was like a 2yr old she wanted this and that, thank God Janice had control, she picked up what she wanted and we were out of there.

By then it was time to pick up Roger from therapy. Janice took Roger home and then we ladies hit Wall Mart store. Where Gale picked out a watch and I picked out some sweat pants and socks for my operation, we came home and lounged around. Janice had to hem she said she didn't mind. Had supper, Watched TV till 12am, and then went to bed.

Next day it was time to take a shower and get ready to go back home. We went to Eat and Park for lunch and then we came home. I went to Gales to see all her gifts, and then they brought me home. I had a nice time at Pastor Forry and Janice, They made my Christmas took my mind off myself and my brother and my mother, but then coming home it was back to reality.

Christmas 2013 was as good as good to be expected without my brother may he rest in peace and may he continue to watch over me.

How Did I Bring 2014 In?

And we had our usual kolbossie and sourkaurt and a little later we had cheese it wasn't much excitement, but it was fun. Gale my best friend stayed overnight and we ate cheese and crackers and meat. You see where I live you can't make a lot of noise or they call the police. People from 55 and up to 90 yrs. old live here so I can understand.

So Gale and I just watch TV and listen to my two new CDS. And then when 9:45 rolled around the Point Stadium put fireworks off, Gale and I enjoyed them, we just had to look out my living room window, they were nice but they weren't as good as last year's 2013, Gale was like a kid saying ooh and ah. After they were finished Gale said she was going to bed.

I stayed up to watch the ball drop, I have to admit I dozed off here and there, but I did see the ball drop and off to bed I went.

So you see we did bring in the NEW YEAR 2014 Quietly. I made a new year's resolution to give up sugar I did once before and I can do it again.

I Started the New Year Off
On the Wrong Foot
1-25-14

Some may question why I say that. Well my answer is that on Jan 14th 2014 I had hernia surgery, the doctor told Helen and Gale everything went well. I came home the same day, talk about pain I couldn't move it hurt when I coughed, or moved. I was taking Percocet every four hrs. Helen made phone calls to my family, and my other support team who were concerned about me. Gale my best friend took care of me by making meals doing dishes, helping me in and out of bed, getting the shower water temp right so I could wash myself, Gale dried me off and then she would put a fresh bandage over my incision. Then she would help dress me, by then I was tired.

When I first saw my incision I was really upset it looked discussing I hated myself. Gale also helped washed my cloths Went for groceries, and the credit union. All I can say is Gales been a big help and support I don't know what I would have done without her.

When it came time to go to the doctors Gale ask her friend Sharon from church if she would take us to the doctors and she did, so I want to thank her for doing that. The doctor took the strips stitches off and put three new ones on. I have to go back in two wks. I still look discussing. Gale is staying with me till Thursday 1-30-14. I don't understand why I still have pain, but I'll just take a pain pill.

Don't know how I can ever pay Gale for what's she's done for me, but give me time and I'll think of something.

I hope soon my self-esteem will come back, and I'll be feeling good as new, until then I just have to deal with it. Recovery takes time.

Missing My Dad
2-3-14

I don't how to explain it to you dad. But today is your anniversary that you've been gone I don't recall how many years that your gone but it seems just like today, it's so fresh in my mind I can't help it. I still see you walking into the bank. I can't erase it from my mind I'm sorry.

Today is just a sad day for me, yes there will be tears shed and yes that's okay. I'll be crying for two reasons not just you but John passed away on September 3rd. What makes those days so memorable is it pay day for me on the 3rd.

I try to think of happy times we had together and dad it's our walks we took to town and back home.

John it's time we spent looking at your trains

One thing I have to say is I take after you is I tolerate pain like you and John I had a hernia for over 2 years and finally had surgery, I had a lot of pain I tried not to take pain pills I know how you were dad and John.

Well today I'll just have to take it minute by minute. May you both rest in peace.

Life
2-10-14

In my first book I wrote about life and now in my 2nd book I'm going to mention about my life again. Some of it may be repeated.

Life has thrown me another curve and I haven't adjusted to it very well. One of the curves is my hernia surgery I'm having some problems dealing with the recovery process and the pain that goes with it, and the limitations. People or I should say my support team say I'm strong, well there wrong I have a lot of anger inside of me and the voices keep telling me to just take a knife to my stomach and cut it all open and end my life. Now you tell me is that being strong.

I want to take my anger out on Pat my therapist who I haven't seen for over a month but that's not fair to her, but if she says I did well for the length of time I may have to show her my anger.

I had another curve thrown at me I lost my volunteering job at the church. I'm not taking that well either, I really like that job there was no pressure, doing that I felt like a somebody, now I feel like a person who needs to reach out to a support team to face life's challenges that come my way. I'm not strong I may put on a face that I am, but deep inside I'm hurting,

The curves Gods giving me now I'm finding it hard to deal with, so support team you know who are, give me guidance and help it would be greatly appreciated till I get back on my two feet again and be able to face life challenges that come my way.

Thank You Sincerely
Loretta

Some Places I Can Go To Get A Smile
3-4-14

You sometimes stop and wonder or think why would I have to look for a smile? Well it has to do with my mental illness, which causes me to have mood swings that go up and down and the voices I hear almost every day.

So when I'm blue and want to reach out for that smile I go to the credit union to see Sharon, Marybeth, Ruth, Connie, they tease me about going into the fountain in central park I tell them I'm out of commission since I had my surgery. But there very nice to me, they just know what to say to put a smile on my face for the day.

Another place I sometimes walk to is the Lee Shoppe the ladies are always nice to me there. Marie or Linda wait on me if they have a chance to talk they do, Marlene usually before she starts work always comes to talk to me and Maries sister she's a cook always pops her head out to say hi and how you doing, and then there's Norma she's always running around.

Someone one else I talk to is my best friend Gale I call her every day or she calls me. She's always sending me cards to cheer me up or brighten up my day. Sundays we go to McDonalds and then visit my mom.

And then there's my friend Debbie I talk to her when I'm feeling blue I don't call her a lot because its long distance, but when I do call she helps me out. By the end of the call she has me laughing As for my family I talk to Barb, Ken, and Annamarie. We have some fun conversation, but mostly serious stuff. Oh I almost forgot Irene and Dorothy they know how to cheer me up, I don't get them only once a month, but when I do they are always happy to see me. I can't let out Sheryl from Dr. Bach office. She's always sending me caring cards and I do the same, she is a very nice person. So are Sharon and Ronnette there nice to. I'm sorry how could I forget Pastor Roger Forry. He's a great person and friend of mine. I've only known him for a couple of years but if you want a good laugh talk to him. He can make you laugh on the phone and in person. He's also a kind and caring and loving person. So thanks a lot Pastor Roger Forry. Janice Forry is a good person to. When I have a problem she will try to help me she comes down and gets Gale and me and takes us up to her and Roger's house. We have a good time. We do things. So thank you Janice. I'm not going to leave these three people who play an important part of my life. I may cry in the beginning but by the end I have a smile they are Pat, Helen Megan So you see I reach out to a lot of people for one little smile, but that smile can go a long way.

Pain
3-8-14

Right now my resource of pain comes from my operation on my hernia that I had on Jan 14-2014. I could deal with pain form before my operation. But now that I've had the operation my levels of pain from a 10 to 5 once in a while I may hit a 3. I'm not dealing with it to good. I try hard not to complain, sometimes times I hide the pain very well, and other times it shows on my face. I thought once I had the surgery I wouldn't have any pain.

I control my pain with pain pills, the problem with that is I can't take them if I'm going to drive. Otherwise I take one pain pill every 4 to 6 hours and lay on the couch with moist heat in the evening, I don't like it.

When I went to the doctors they said it would take at least 3 months to fully recover and some recover quicker than others. I often think of my dad he hated to take pills, I'm the same way when it comes to pain medication. So when I do take a pain pill I say to myself here's to you dad enjoy, and let the medication do its thing.

Motivation
3-13-14

I think everybody needs motivation at some point in their life. For example the spirit motivates me to write stories at night like when I'm ready to go to bed, and then I have to get up and start writing.

Another example for me is just to wake up in the morning and get out of bed to start a new day. I recall when I was in my 30's I was a runner I ran every morning that's how I got motivated to started my day. I ran for 3 reasons one just to get out of bed, two to lose weight, three to help lift my depression all three work.

Other people that have a job get motivated by having their first cup of coffee and going to the gym to work out before they go to work; some just need that one cigarette.

Maybe I shouldn't say this about my friend Gale, she has a problem doing dishes but what gets her motivated is when she's expecting someone like Janice Forry or her case worker, then she's full speed ahead. She also makes time to do her meditation.

Motivation is a good thing that happens to most of us.

Stress
3-16-14

Stress in general plays important part in my life. It all started when I was growing up as a child. All I heard was do this or do that don't go there. I had racing thoughts, and heard voices to harm myself, I'd cut myself, I'd never hurt anyone even though the person hurt me.

I mentioned in my first book after I graduated I finally went for help. I was hospitalized three times for suicidal thoughts. I haven't been in the hospital for at least twenty or more years. I've had some good therapist but Pat Hydock been the best. She helps me cope with my stress and so does Helen, and my support team.

What causes me stress just everyday living, getting up and starting a new day. I'm getting a little better at saying when I get it by saying when I get up in the morning and say I'm going to try my best to have a good day.

When it comes to the beginning of the month and its time to pay bills and write out checks it stresses me out because I'm not sure my check book is balanced. But I solved that because Marybeth, Ruth, Sharon, Connie from the credit union balance my check book.

I'm always stressing over my weight, but I'm working on that by cutting out sugar. I stress over my car because of the year it is and I don't know if I have enough money to get another one so I keep praying it will keep running

Another thing I stress over is my mom. I know she's being taking care of at the nursing home, but some day she's not going to be there.

When I hear the voices and there strong I cope by listening to music, go for a walk talk to Gale or other support people, or pray. That one thing

I do every night before I go to bed I pray the rosary, I don't only pray for myself I pray for my family and friends.

I know I'm not the only one that has stress in my life, but they just with it differently.

Pain is another stressor I had surgery Jan 14th 2014 I still have pain. I'm dealing with it the best way I can.

I Take a Look in the Mirror
4-12-14

Tonight after a rough day I'm taking a look in the mirror. I'm asking myself what I see. My answer to that is I'm a 55yr old woman striving hard with everyday living, facing facts about my mom going downhill and seeing her that way hurts. I work hard on losing weight every day.

I see an unhappy person dealing with voices in my head every day. I'd like to see someone else in my shoes like a member of my family and see how they would cope with it.

I'm a caring person that even if I'm busy and one of my friends or family needs help I drop everything and go and help them. I've been told to put myself first but I find that hard to do. Just like saying the word no, is another one.

When I wake up in the morning and look in the mirror I try to tell myself I'm going to have a good day. So when I go out for a walk when I see someone on the street I'll tell them good morning and if I'm talking to someone I'll tell them have a good day.

I'm a woman in pain and learning to cope with it the best way possible with pain pills.

Helen has me working on goals right now. How to be a friend, Happiness, Gratitude, and positive things, and working toward recovery.

Pat and I work on my depression, life in general, and suicidal thoughts, and grief.

So maybe when I get up tomorrow and look in the mirror I'll have a better attitude and won't be so scared and be happy and even have a smile on my face its worth a try that's all I can do and say.

Coping
4-12-14

Coping with life is a challenge for me. For others it's just another day and they don't have a care in the world.

For me it's a vicious cycle up and down that's what schizoaffective disorder is, never an even keel that's the problem. Hearing voices don't help it just makes this all the harder to cope with.

How am I coping with it, I pray the rosary every night, listen to music, watch TV, work on my cross stitch, go for a walk, or do something nice for myself, talk to a friend, talk to Pat, Helen, Megan, or my other support team, that's all my resources which is enough.

Not everyone has these options like I do. So I'm grateful for the services and my friends.

My brother John passed away on September 3rd 2013. I miss him very much, I was so used to calling him at 12:30pm and now there's a void. My way of coping with that is crying or leave my apartment. They tell me crying is good for me.

On January 14th 2014 I had hernia surgery. My best friend Gale helped take care of me. Helen took me for the surgery but Gale and her friend took me to the doctors. Gale was very helpful; I took pills around the clock. Since surgery I still have pain, I'm a strong person when it comes to pain. I take oxycodone every 4 to 6 hours I'm very careful with it I only take it when I need it. So that's how I'm coping with that, there are days I cry.

With my mom Gale and I go to visit her on Sundays and I may go one day during the week. Gale goes to support me without her I don't know what I'd do, she helps keep me in control again I sometimes cry and sometimes have anger.

Crowds are another problem, Helen is helping me with that, we go to McDonalds at different times and when it gets crowed I try to stay as long as I can or until it gets too much for me, then we leave. Same way going for groceries I go and get out.

I don't go to church anymore because of how crowed the mass gets, so I solved the problem the priest comes to my apt, and I receive communion every first Friday of the month so that's less stress for me.

so you see some of the things I've written down is everyday living, some more are is just trying to get out of bed, I have to have a reason to get out of bed, if I see the sun shining that gives me a purpose. I know I have to take care of my hygiene go for a walk and treat myself to breakfast, someone else it wouldn't matter it's just another day. With the weather breaking I hope to get out of the rut I'm in. I'll be going for more walks, try to get rid of the pain I'm having. I keep telling myself someone else has it worse off than me, keep up with what I'm doing, and hang in there, better days are ahead.

Losing my mom
4-30-14

I lost my mom on April 22, 2014 I wanted to spend her last days with her, it was hard on me watching her but it was also important to me. I need the closer time. She had seven children, so it was time to give back.

I realize I might have been wrong by telling her to hang on till I come back, because I and my friend would leave to go eat or go home for a little bit.

But finally my sister Barb told me I should tell her it's okay to let go. I came to my senses I got close to my mom and told her she could let go that I'd be okay, that I'd be okay. I don't know which was harder telling her to let go or watching her die for a day and half and knowing I'll never see her again.

Now it's time to remember the good times. For instance holidays, my mom would go all out food and presents. She would be the last one to sit down at the table because she wanted to make sure everyone had something to eat, we would have to tell her to sit down. At Christmas time she would play Santa clause and hand out all the gifts, she had a good time. She hasn't been able to do that for 5yrs it's just a memory.

She enjoyed quilting, She loved flowers every memorial day her and I would go to the cemetery's and plant flowers on the graves, she ask me if something happened to her if I would take care of the graves, I promised her I would.

She lived with my sister Barb for 1yr. and we joked with her because her speech was going when you would ask her a question her response would be yes and then no then you would have to ask her which is it yes or no. My sister had nurses come in and help out. But her dementia was progressing, so the next move was a nursing home.

She lived at the Presbyterian Home for 4yrs. My friend Gale and I would visit her as much as possible, I would go by myself it was hard but I did it. Even though she couldn't talk she knew the family. She had a feeding tube in her.

She put up a hard fight, but she's not suffering any more. She's at a better place now.

How My Mom Would Want Me To Remember Her?
5-15-14

When I take the time to sit down and think about her she didn't have an easy life. Seriously now, she had seven children, and times were rough. But between my mom and dad they made sure there was food on the table and clothes on our backs. My mom had asthma real bad. She always made sure I was clean for school and church on Sundays. She taught me manners to say no thank you and please, yes mom and no mom and dad whatever the case would be.

She was a happy person. When she had a chance to get out of the house, she did. She took care of her mother, until she passed away at the age of 95.

She had a problem with her weight, but she worked on it by going to Tops. It got her out and she had fun with the ladies. I would try to help her by going to the track and walking. We did it a couple of times, but then she would give up and quit.

My mom belonged to the ladies' guild from our church. She would always cook the dinners. It was hard work, but it was something she enjoyed.

We went to basket parties together. We went to Pizza Hut on Tuesday nights for their buffet. We took turns paying. On Sundays we would go up to my sister Barbs for dinner. My mom was in charge of the desserts, and I was in charge of the vegetables. That gave her a chance to see her grandchildren.

Christmas was a fun time. I enjoyed helping my mom prepare for Christmas Eve dinner, and then she played Santa Claus handing out the gifts to the kids and grown-ups.

The other thing my mom and I would do together was to plant flowers at the cemetery. I made a promise to her I'd take care of them when she couldn't.

My mom went on a few bus trips. She also took the train to see my sister, Tammy and her family for Thanksgiving.

I remember my sister, Barb taking my mom down to Virginia Beach to see my brother a couple of times, and when she'd go I'd take care of her cats and mail.

So you see I want to remember my mom leading a full productive and happy life, not her spending 4 years in the Presbyterian home.

How Hard It Is Coming Down From a High
7-13-14

I'm speaking from experience, I don't mean street drugs. I'm talking about a weekend vacation. I haven't been on a vacation for at least 10yrs or more. Well I take that back I've gone to Pastor Forry and Janice Forry. But this time Janice Forry Gale and I went out of town it was just one day to my brother Ken and Kathleen's place in Lanacastor.

My brother took us sightseeing to the Amish places like the quilting places, toy place, Gale thought it was amazing, I thought so to, Gale was like a child oh this and oh that, she wanted to buy everything.

I was amazed how they walk the street with no shoes on. And how many buggies we saw on the street, and also they cut grass with the old type lawn mowers. I also enjoyed looking at all the quilts. I think Janice enjoyed herself to.

Ken and Kathleen took us out to eat at this Amish restaurant, they really had the food there, and then for dessert they stop at this ice cream place where they make ice cream.

We went back to the house and sat out on the deck until it started to storm. We moved inside and sat in the sitting room and talk. As it got late Janice and Gale went upstairs to bed, but I stayed down stairs for a while and talk a little more to Ken and Kathleen.

Before I forget all day Ken and Kathleen kept in contact with their daughter Kristine., who was working on a hard case that she couldn't come home, she works in a group home with two autistic boys they were short staff and no one could come to the hospital to relieve Kristine so she kept in contact with her mom and dad while we were there

Now I went to bed and slept till eight o'clock took a shower and waited for Gale and Janice to wake up. When they did wake up they took their showers and then we had breakfast. We talked a little bit and then we said our good byes.

Janice took Gail and I to some out let stores we had fun shopping. Then Janice took us to lunch.

Janice surprised us with 2 tickets to Sights and Sounds, a play about Moses I really enjoyed that. They had real live animals and the characters did a good job to. After that we went to the Olive Garden to eat supper that was good to.

Then we headed on our journey back home. We didn't get home until ten fifteen. Pastor Forry seemed happy to see us. We came home and the couch and one chair was gone, the reason for that was Janice and Roger were getting new carpeting in the living room and dining room.

We went to bed and slept till eight thirty took a shower had breakfast, talk a little bit, and then Janice said she was ready to go.

Now it was time to face reality something I wasn't looking forward to. But the sooner you face it the better I guess the better it is.

Well it was all good while it lasted; I'm now off my high. If you have to deal with and face what I deal with you will understand. It's not just mental illness it's a number of things. Some of you know. Lord help me get through this.

Fighting
7-28-14

No I don't mean boxing or wrestling. I mean fighting to live every day. I understand that my brother John was fighting for his life battling cancer. And I think my mom put up a good fight till the end. I really think she gave up when I told her I'd be okay and that she could go because it was shortly after I told her that she was gone.

But now I'm speaking for myself. I'm constantly battling mental illness. It's no joke. When I went to my last dr. appointment I told nurse Becky I can't fight anymore and her response was she's known me for 12yrs and I keep fighting even though I tell her I'm tired of fighting. Little do people know I will get tired of fighting and give up the ship and the boat is going to sink. With or without a no harm contract because I won't be in my right mind. The fight with the voices will no longer be a problem, and no more pain, no more worries.

Just Peace of Mind.

My Birthday Turning 56
8-18-14

Mostly my friends and support team and family know how hard my birthdays are for me. It's not just that big of a deal as the number. I'm not happy on that day; I already know I'm not going to have a birthday cake.

I look back at 55 to see the things I've accomplished and what has happened to me over that period of time.

Well on Sept 3rd 2013 my oldest brother passed away. And then on April 22nd, 2014 my mom passed away. So it's been a rough road for me with the grieving process. I'm working on it.

My birthday is coming up in less than a week. I'm having a mass said for my brother, John on the 23rd my birthday. So I'll be celebrating death and also life that day. I hope you understand where I'm coming from.

But now it's time to step back and look at what I've accomplished at 55. I finished paying on my burial plot for when I die, and now I'm working on stone. I don't want that burden on my brothers and sisters when I die. I want to be more independent in that way. I'm working on my 2nd book.

On Jan14, 2014 I had hernia surgery. Helen, my Peer Star person and Gale took me for it. They were a big help with my recovery. My family and friends called to see how I was doing from time to time. Now I have a small hernia. I went for therapy and they put me on a tens machine. That works. So I invested into one of them and do it twice a day, if possible, to relieve the pain, and I take less pain medication.

I'm still going to see Pat Hydock for therapy twice a month and still signing no harm contracts.

I'm still able to keep up my hygiene, clean my apartment, continue to pay my bills on time, work on a budget, take care of a car, do a lot of praying, and to deal with my anger. I go for brisk walks and pay for it later, take care of my medication, and work on my weight.

While I was still 55 Mrs. Forry took Gale and I down to Lancaster to see my brother. We had a nice time.

So you see for me birthdays aren't always blowing out candles on a cake, or just a number.

I'm trying hard to move on with my life for what I've been through; I hope 56 is better than 55.

Thinking About You John
8-26-14

It's 11:30 pm Monday night and you are in my thoughts and prayers. Just want to write down some things about you, that other people would like to know about you that they didn't know and to get it off my chest.

For starters you were my big brother, and I always looked up to you. I could depend on you. Growing up when you got your first job, and received your first pay check, you bought chips for us younger brothers and sisters. That was a real treat. You always seemed to look out for us. You liked trains and sports. You were an altar boy until you graduated from high school. You joined the Army and were stationed in different places, but the one place that stands out the most is Alaska. You disliked that place, and you were there for 3 years. As I recall you sent a dog home from there. It was a Malamute Husky. When you were discharged, you came back home and lived with mom and dad. That was okay with them.

I was still living at home and wanted to learn how to drive. I was still in school. You tried to teach me once or twice, but couldn't handle it. I ended up taking driver's ED through school.

You got a job at Lee Hospital and worked there for a long time and worked at Roseland Bingo a couple nights a week. One thing about you John, you were a hard worker, I have to say that. You or Ken, my other brother, would take turns cutting grass at the house.

I think, I'm not sure how old you were, when you moved out of the house, you bought a house of your own.

And then a couple years later you met Janet and married her. She had a son of her own, and that was your family. As time went by you still loved your trains. You always had a display at Christmas time.

After a couple years you and Janet sold your house and moved into a ranch house. It's beautiful and it's what you both wanted. You had your own train room display. You were working at Memorial Hospital for a long time with them.

You were a busy man, trying to take care of your business and mom's business when she got sick and some of my business. Then you became ill it was time we take care of you. You suffered, John, and you put up a fight. I keep that in my mind. But you were my big brother, and you looked out for me in different ways. I'll never forget you, and I'll always keep you in my prayers. I love you. God bless you.

Dealing with Mental Illness and Losing Weight Is A CONSTANT Battle
2-20-15

Some may say, so what, but I say, oh shit. I wish I could get rid of them both. It's an everyday constant battle. Like I had said in my first book I have a label for my mental illness. It's called schizoaffective. That's when you have mood swings like highs and lows. Sometimes I might have a day or two on an even keel, but that's rarely. Same way with the voices and seeing things I can go a day.

But how do I take care of it? With medication every day and every night. I try to tell myself one day I'll wake up, and it will all go away, but I'm only fooling myself. My mental illness is something that can be treated but not cured.

Now move on to losing weight. I blame some of it on the medication I'm taking, and the other I blame on myself. As of 2 wks. Ago Helen and I put me on an exercise program and diet food. I'm making progress. I've lost some weight, but the thing is that you have to stay in control like what you eat and drink and exercise. I'm not saying it's easy. It's a constant battle that will stick with me the rest of my life.

Who Am I?
3-10-15

From time to time throughout the year I ask myself that question, and it changes a little bit. So, let's see, who am I? I turned 56 on Aug. 23, 2014. I have aches and pains, maybe more than other 56 year olds. I deal with it the best way I can. I can cope with pain without taking one of stronger pills until I'm almost crying. I try not to talk about it. I use a tension unit every night before I go to bed to ease the pain on my hernia. I pray the rosary also, which helps.

With my situation with my mental illness, if it wasn't for Pat, my therapist, Helen, Cassey, Gale, Debbie, Dianne, and other support I wouldn't be here. They have given me coping skills and goals to work on. It hasn't been an easy road. I've wanted to throw in the towel many times. I lost my brother, John in the year 2013, and lost my mom in the year 2014. I talked about wanting to take my own life, but I didn't. I had a good support team.

Also in the year 2014 I had to make a big decision and decide to get a new car. I'm able to continue to keep up with all my bills and still have some spending money.

I've come out of my shell a little more. I made some more friends that I sit downstairs some evenings, and we talk, but I make sure I come back up to my apartment at 8:00 pm.

Helen helped me get on an exercise program and healthy eating to lose weight. I'm doing well I think.

With my mental health, in the back of my head I still want to die. The voices are still with me, and I don't know what to do to change it.

Looking back on this, I'm Loretta Knapp who been through a lot, but has a support team to back me up when times are good and bad, no matter what. So she just has to hang in there. God's not ready for her yet.

Birthdays
8-24-15

For me it makes me look back on last year, I have to cry because it's so hard to face a new day. Looking back I had to face losing my brother 2yrs ago which is hard and losing my mother 1yr ago which is hard to.

Every year I face the obstacle of losing weight something good has come out it I've gone from a size 16 pants to a size 12, I never ate so much chicken, fish, hamburger, yogurt, and water as I do now. I also walk down ten flight of stairs a day, and do plenty of walking. I have friends at night we walk the garage. So you see it's an obstacle and yet it's a challenge.

I had to get a new car. I still have Gale and Debbie as my best friends, and now I made some new friends, I'm the youngest one in the group. They support me when I'm down and so do some of my members of my family

Believe it or not my friends have me playing bingo, I win sometimes and lose sometimes it works on my nerves but the money I win I'm saving for Christmas.

Health wise I'm giving up no more doctors, I'll just have to live on my psych meds and pain medicine, and my tension unit no complaining any more. I'll still talk to Pat and Helen and hang around my support team.

I'm also trying hard to work on my story book to get published this year. Helen and Gale are helping with that.

I guess you can say I've overcome some obstacles this year and challenges I'm still independent, pay my bills, keep my apartment clean, and my hygiene. And I think I'm improving when I want something I go after it with Helen and Pats approval. I made changes with my life. If only I could get rid of the voices and depression and suicidal thoughts
Happy Birthday to Me

My Journey
9-11-15

I think and feel God gave us all a journey in life. Mine has been dealing with mental illness, which is depression, being schizoaffective, that's when you have highs and lows, ups and downs like a roller coaster.

The journey can be a challenging like losing my brother John and my mom that was a double wammy, I'm coping with the best way I can. I have Pat, Helen, Gale, Megan, Debbie, and other support people. I know I have to go through the grieving process and I'm not just going to forget them.

Another challenge was looking for a car, picking the right price range, and in good condition. Helen and I managed to do that together. I think we did a good job.

Accepting the fact that my friend Martha is in a nursing home that part doesn't bother me it's just she's so far away and I won't be able to visit as often.

MY journey in life has me work on goals with Helen like becoming organized, coping skills with stress, health issues, Communications skills, choices and many more.

Every day I face a challenge as to whether I want to get out of bed or not and what I have to look for into today, I have that choice to make.

God gave me this cross road journey buy I'm learning from it and growing. My mental illness plays a part in my journey, but I try not to let it get in the way. I'll never know when my journey will end. So may God be with you when you start your journey and may he be there at the end of your journey. God Bless

Loretta

Every day I face a challenge as to whether this book to help other people with mental illness, And to cope with their illness whatever it maybe and to encourage them to go on living.

There's is help out there as I expressed it in this book.

It's very helpful to have a strong support team you can turn to. I wrote this book from my own experiences hope you enjoy reading this book and find it helpful.

Printed in the United States
By Bookmasters